WELCOME

It can be overwhelming and time-consuming to prepare for public speaking events. They can be so dynamic and you have no idea what you're stepping into. The Remarkable Framework gives you the confidence to speak in dynamic situations with the support of reliable tools and eliminates the agonizing over lengthy drafts and writer's block.

In the sections of this workbook, I've compiled all the framework tools you need to improve your speaking skills and structure any real-world speaking situation. You'll get access to the drills, worksheets, and videos that augment the training available in the chapters in my book, *Remarkable Speaking: A Framework to Embody Your Voice and Your Vision.* You'll also learn how to use my time-saving framework. It's designed to help you articulate what you want to say and structure any speaking event in minutes, whether it be a speech, presentation, pitch, webinar, seminar, podcast, facilitation, meeting agenda, employee training, lunch and learn, moderating panel discussions, recording videos, interviews, social media posts, and yes, so much more!

The Remarkable Framework will become your go-to public speaking solution. Use it routinely to step into your power and truly embody what it means to be a remarkable speaker. It's like having a coach in your pocket!

Your coach,

Remarkable Speaking Workbook
A time-saving framework to help you articulate and structure any speaking event—in minutes!

remarkablespeaking.com

Copyright © 2025 Shelley Goldstein

Published by Made to Change the World™ Publishing
Nashville, TN

Cover and interior design by Elizabeth Baldwin

ISBN: 978-1-956837-55-1 Paperback

Printed in the USA, Canada, Australia, and Europe

CONTENTS

TONGUE TWISTERS

Tongue twisters help to improve pronunciation, confidence and focus. When you concentrate on pronouncing the nonsense words quickly and repeatedly, there is little time to overthink and deliberate their association. The more you focus on saying the words while practicing the Tongue Twister and Say What?! drills, the more you'll get into flow and embody confidence.

Tongue Twister Drill

Repeat the following tongue twister until you can pronounce each word without fumbling. It may take you a few rounds, but stick with it. Because this is a speaking drill, say it out loud.

The thirty-three thieves thrilled the throne with thistles through Thursday.

PRO TIP: Focus on a clear pronunciation at a slower pace before increasing your speed. Once you can say it correctly slowly, gradually pick up the pace.

More tongue twisters:

- Give papa a cup of proper coffee in a copper coffee cup.
- Scissors sizzle, thistles sizzle.
- Cross a coarse cow across a crowded cow crossing carefully.
- A skunk sat on a stump and thunk the stump stunk, but skunk stunk.
- Betty bought some butter to make her batter better but the butter was bitter.
- The swan swam over the sea; swim, swan, swim!
- No need to light a night-light on a light night like tonight.
- How can a clam cram in a clean cream can?
- Persnickety penguins packed a picnic of plum and pickle pies.

Say What?! Drill

For this tongue twister variation, choose one ridiculous word from the list that follows and repeat it two times. The first time, speak the word with commanding force as if it's the most important thing you have to say. The second time, speak the word with doubt as if you question what you're saying.

1. Commanding force: **Bumfuzzle!**
2. Doubt: *Bumfuzzle?*

PRO TIP: To speak with commanding force is to have strong intent as if you're pounding really hard on a drum. To speak with doubt is to have a shaky feeling as if you are walking on a tightrope thirty feet above the ground.

Notice the contrast. Think about the two styles of speaking; how would you describe your feeling each time? Which style felt more empowering? Which one left room for uncertainty? The commanding force is what confidence feels like. There's no doubting it when you say

"Bumfuzzle!"

More ridiculous words:

- Jabberwocky
- Snickersnee
- Fubsy
- Collywobbles
- Taradiddle
- Omnishambles
- Cattywampus
- Spondulicks
- Diphthong
- Finifugal

BOX BREATHE

Box breathing is a drill to maintain the rest-and-digest state in your body when you start to feel anxious or uncomfortable before a speaking event. It is often used by the United States Navy Seals and professional and amateur athletes, and is recommended by medical practitioners to reduce stress, restore calm, and get the excitable adrenaline and grounding dopamine pumping.

When box breathing, it's important to inhale as deeply as you exhale. You will feel a difference in just four cycles, but don't just think about breathing. I want you to feel cyclones of air moving around in your body. Maybe your shoulders rise with a big nourishing inhale. Maybe you feel a sigh of relief as your chest collapses on the exhale. The idea is to breathe as if you're filling every cell in your body with oxygen.

Follow these step-by-step instructions, or scan the QR code below to watch my guided video on box breathing on the Remarkable Framework YouTube playlist (youtube.com/ @remarkablespeaking).

 Box Breathing

Sit comfortably in a chair or a crossed-legged position on the floor.

Whatever phone calls, to-do lists, and emails are filling your inbox, put them all in a jar. Now put the jar on the other side of the door. I promise you, it'll be there when you're done with this drill.

Visualize a box like the diagram on page 4. Follow the arrows around the four sides of the box, inhaling, holding, and exhaling for four counts on each side. Repeat this cycle four times.

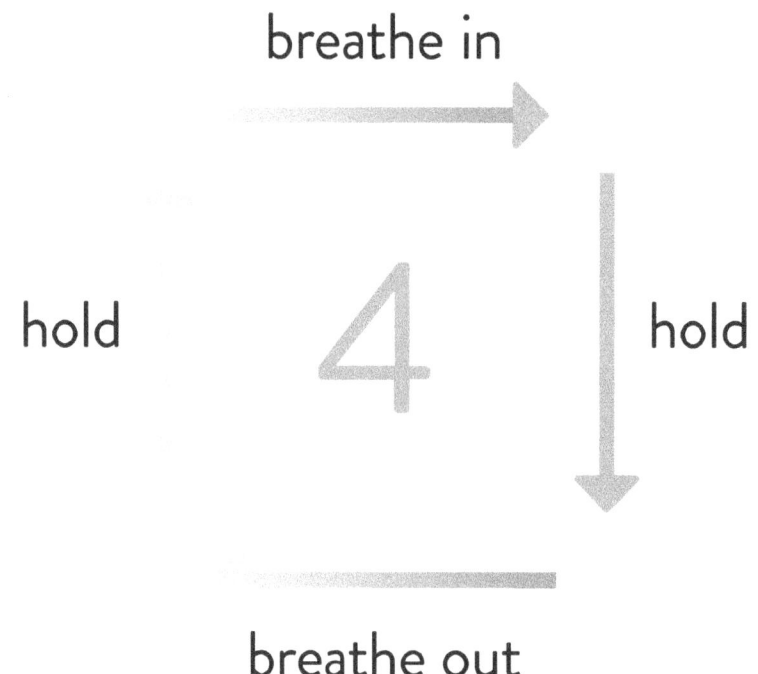

breathe in

hold   4   hold

breathe out

1. Breathe in for four long and steady counts.

2. Hold the breath in for four steady counts.

3. Breathe out for four long and steady counts.

4. Hold the breath out for four counts, long and steady.

PRO TIP: As you breathe, visualize the movement of ocean waves. With each inhale, fill your body like the incoming tide of waves crashing onto the shore. With each exhale, release your breath like the outgoing tide as it recedes into the ocean. The holding of the breath is like the moment of suspension when the wave changes direction.

When you've completed the box breathing experience, consider how you feel. Has there been a shift in your body? Do you feel more relaxed?

BREATHE POST-IT®

Taking a breath is your all-around, good-at-anytime way to find calm. The breath recharges your brain, and your speaking will have more clarity.

So you don't forget to breathe when you're speaking, write the word **BREATHE** on a Post-it®, and stick it on your computer or at the top of your to-do list. Alternatively, scan the QR code below to download the following image and use it as your screensaver.

SPEAKING OPPORTUNITIES

From a casual chat to participating in virtual webinars, small interactions can help you to improve your confidence and practice public speaking. There are Zoom calls, meetings, team reviews, networking events and collaborations with colleagues where you can initiate a conversation. These conversations can be in-person or online—they all count as opportunities to speak.

Set a one-minute timer and, using the worksheet on page 8, list three opportunities to speak or converse in the next twenty-four hours. For example:

- Raise your hand during a webinar with a simple "Thank you."
- Go to a cafe and say, "Hello" to the person sitting next to you.
- Show your support for a colleague with clapping gestures on your next Zoom call.
- Ask a Lyft or bus driver, "How are things looking around town today?"
- Comment on a social media post, "Interesting, I learned something new!"

PRO TIP: If the opportunity feels scary, box breathe to relax.

PRO TIP: Once you've made your list, take action and speak up!

SPEAKING OPPORTUNITIES WORKSHEET

Opportunity 1

Opportunity 2

Opportunity 3

Opportunity 1

Opportunity 2

Opportunity 3

Opportunity 1

Opportunity 2

Opportunity 3

ICEBREAKERS

Icebreakers help you to connect with your audience and cultivate a comfortable environment. As a speaker, you're the meeting host, and that's your opportunity to set the tone and create the experience you want. Introduce a few of the following icebreakers at your next meeting.

- Ask about the biggest challenge they are facing in the industry right now.
- Present a "this or that" question: Do they prefer the city or the countryside?
- You just read an article about the latest industry news. Ask someone how it relates to their business.
- Let them know you're eager to know if there are any breakthroughs or challenges with a project.
- Tell people you're reading a book to improve your speaking skills. Ask whether they're attending any professional development workshops.
- Share a famous quote on leadership and ask if they find it inspiring.
- Maybe you just got back from a safari in South Africa. Ask if anyone has traveled there.
- Ask if they can recommend any apps to improve daily productivity.
- Talk about the winning team from a sporting event or the latest series you binged.
- Share a story about your pet and ask if they have pets.

PRO TIP: Hold back judgment and be open to wonderful surprises discovering common interests that you may have with other people.

POWER UP

What maestros, coaches, and instructors all know is that practice creates a routine to form new habits, more opportunities to deliver a great experience, and the freedom to reach your highest potential. Power Up is a four-step drill designed to help you boost your energy and build a routine of speaking with confidence. You can do the drill to warm up before an important call, presentation, or meeting and avoid a shaky start to your opening remarks.

STEP 1: Speak the following tongue twister out loud until you can pronounce each word without fumbling.

No need to light a night-light on a light night like tonight.

Next, speak the following ridiculous word out loud and repeat it two times. The first time, speak the word with commanding force as if it's the most important thing you have to say. The second time, speak the word with doubt as if you question what you're saying.

Commanding force: **Snickersnee!**

Doubt: *Snickersnee?*

STEP 2: Reframe your negative self-talk and take ownership of your ideas and experiences. Ask yourself, "Am I sitting on a chair or a throne?"

STEP 3: Find opportunities to interact! Set a one-minute timer and, on the worksheet that follows, list three potential speaking exchanges in the next twenty-four hours.

SPEAKING OPPORTUNITIES WORKSHEET	
Opportunity 1	
Opportunity 2	
Opportunity 3	

STEP 4: Visualize a box like the diagram below. Follow the arrows around the four sides of the box: breath in for four counts, hold for four, breath out for four counts and hold for four. Repeat this cycle four times to restore calm.

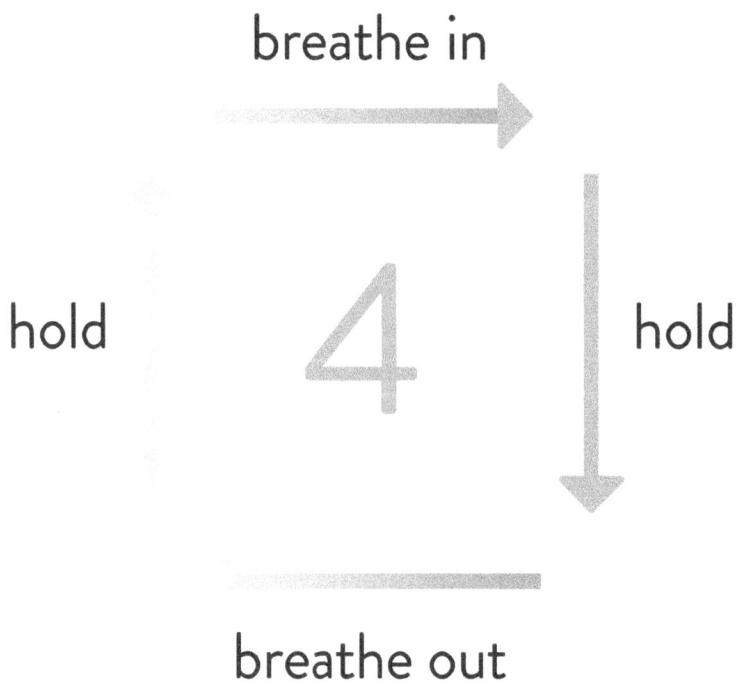

FEELING FINDER

To speak with compassion, there are degrees of emotions and many words for you to use to describe how you feel. The Feeling Finder, my spin on the Plutchik Wheel, can help you understand the range of emotion in the context of speaking.

Pick one of the opportunities you identified on the Speaking Opportunities or Story Bank worksheets in this workbook. Next, using the Feeling Finder on page 14, find two emotions that match the way you felt about that experience.

- First, start in the center of the Feeling Finder and choose one of the six basic emotions.
- Second, look to the middle tier to explore your feelings with more nuance or intensity.
- Third, select from the emotions in the outermost tier to get even more specific.

Now set a timer for one minute and talk about your experience from the perspective of one of the emotions. Set a timer for another minute, repeat the story but from the perspective of the second emotion. Notice how in each perspective of the story, you speak more spontaneously and authentically.

PRO TIP: Looking at the Feeling Finder, ask yourself this question: "How do I feel about that moment?"

PRO TIP: It's okay to experience more than one emotion. The more you can identify your emotions, the better you can manage them and improve your communication with others.

PRO TIP: If you choose to talk about something deeply private, it's important to make sure that you can speak about it with resoluteness and certainty. If not, it may not be a forum to spill your guts.

Choosing words to identify your feelings with the Feeling Finder allows you to manage your reaction, like de-escalating a situation, and communicate your message with less ambiguity.

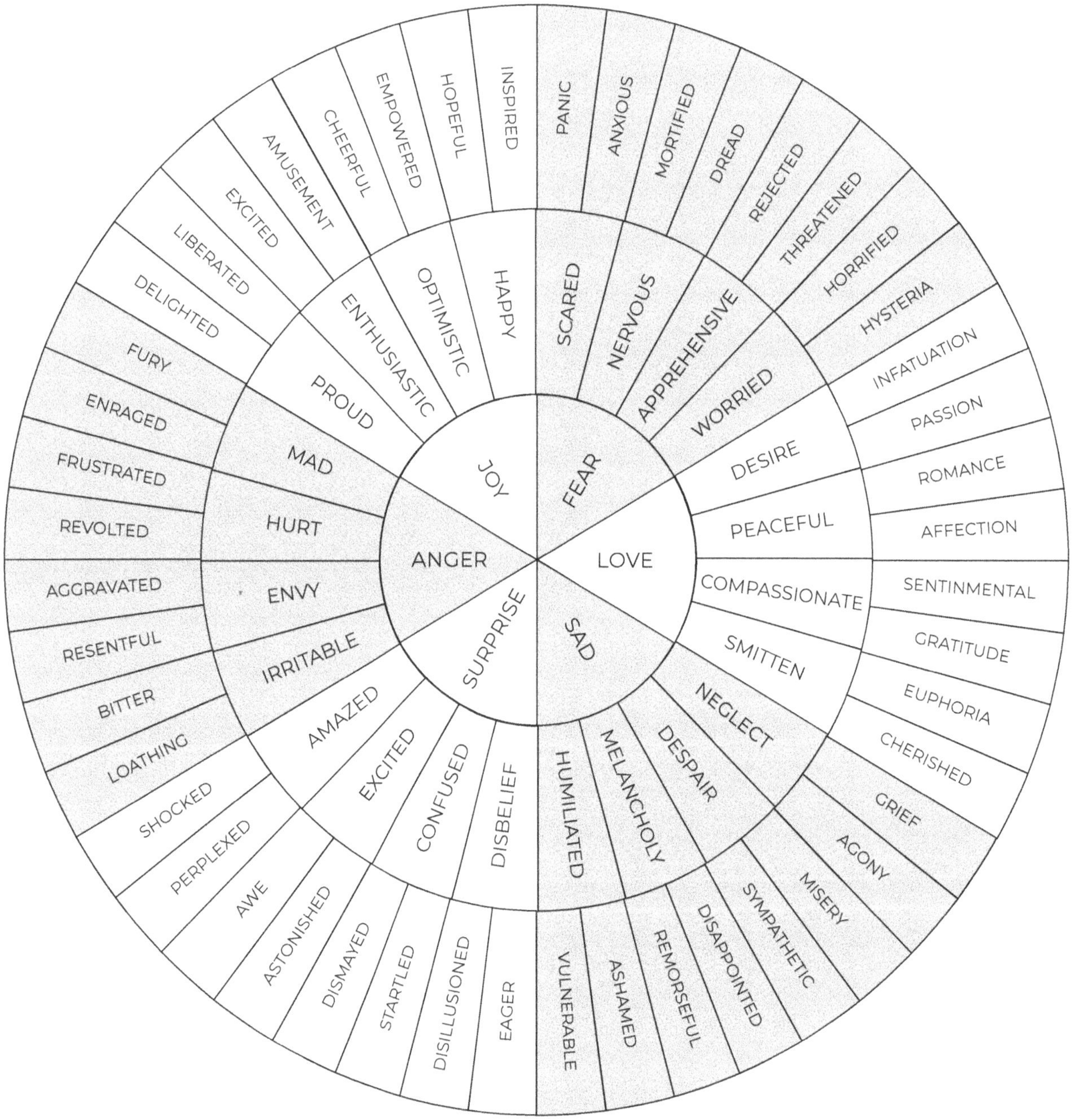

INSPIRED
HOPEFUL
EMPOWERED
CHEERFUL
AMUSEMENT
EXCITED
LIBERATED
DELIGHTED
FURY
ENRAGED
FRUSTRATED
REVOLTED
AGGRAVATED
RESENTFUL
BITTER
LOATHING
SHOCKED
PERPLEXED
AWE
ASTONISHED
DISMAYED
STARTLED
DISILLUSIONED
EAGER
VULNERABLE
ASHAMED
REMORSEFUL
DISAPPOINTED
SYMPATHETIC
MISERY
AGONY
GRIEF
CHERISHED
EUPHORIA
GRATITUDE
SENTINMENTAL
AFFECTION
ROMANCE
PASSION
INFATUATION
HYSTERIA
HORRIFIED
THREATENED
REJECTED
DREAD
MORTIFIED
ANXIOUS
PANIC

HAPPY
OPTIMISTIC
ENTHUSIASTIC
PROUD
MAD
HURT
ENVY
IRRITABLE
AMAZED
EXCITED
CONFUSED
DISBELIEF
HUMILIATED
MELANCHOLY
DESPAIR
NEGLECT
SMITTEN
COMPASSIONATE
PEACEFUL
DESIRE
WORRIED
APPREHENSIVE
NERVOUS
SCARED

JOY
FEAR
LOVE
SAD
SURPRISE
ANGER

VIDEOS: HOW-TO AND MORE

This section includes drills and worksheets for recording video messages and creating multimedia content, along with how-to videos you can watch on the Remarkable Framework YouTube playlist by scanning the QR code below.

One-Take Video Message

Videos are a high-value relationship-building tool and a low-risk way to build your speaking skills. Whether you're communicating via email or in-app message, sending a video message will improve your response rate by sixty percent. Video interactions boost viewers' retention fifty-three percent more than plain text or infographics. When all is said and done, speaking your message is three times faster to convey and results in fewer errors than typing.

To create a video message in seconds, follow these four steps with the One-Take Video Message worksheet on page 16.

Choose an email or text that you need to respond to.

STEP 1: Set a timer for thirty seconds and say—out loud—your one big idea that you want the other person to know.

STEP 2: Write a brief descriptor on the worksheet.

STEP 3: Set a timer for sixty seconds and record your message using your favorite video app.

STEP 4: Post it, share it, send it! It's that fast.

For a demo, watch the One-Take Video on the Remarkable Framework playlist (youtube.com/@remarkablespeaking).

 The One-Take Video

PRO TIP: If you're distracted by looking at yourself on the screen, turn off your self-view when you're recording. Since you don't look at yourself when you're physically in a room with people, I recommend turning off your self-view for any online event and putting yourself in the digital room.

PRO TIP: If you want to engage your audience, before you speak into the camera, ask yourself, "How do I feel about what I'm saying?" Let viewers know you care.

PRO TIP: If you feel uncomfortable, keep recording. With each recording, focus less on the not-so-good videos and be motivated by the good ones.

ONE-TAKE VIDEO MESSAGE WORKSHEET	
Message 1	
Message 2	
Message 3	
Message 4	
Message 5	
Message 6	

Minute Content Creator

Whether you're creating content for your YouTube channel or tutorials to onboard new hires, the Minute Content Creator is my favorite hack to create video content in minutes. You make a list of ten topics and record ten videos in ten minutes. For example, if you're responding to an email about a proposed agenda for an upcoming meeting, list ten key suggestions you'd like the group to consider. If you're creating content for how-to videos, list ten action items or pro tips. If you're pitching a prospect, list ten examples where customers have successfully used your product.

Start by making a list of ten topics using the Minute Content Creator worksheet on page 18. Next, set a timer for one minute and record one topic from your list. Reset the timer for another minute and record a second topic, and continue recording one after the other without stopping. In ten minutes, you'll have ten recordings. Some will be good and some not so good. You might be surprised at how well you actually do. Maybe you get five good recordings, so repeat the exercise and get five more.

PRO TIP: If you feel like you're speaking too fast, manage your energy with a few breaths to slow down.

PRO TIP: If you make a mistake, don't overthink it, keep going to the next recording.

PRO TIP: Your emotions are part of the story, express them to connect with your audience. Ask yourself, "How do I feel about what I'm saying?"

MINUTE CONTENT CREATOR WORKSHEET

Topic 1	
Topic 2	
Topic 3	
Topic 4	
Topic 5	
Topic 6	
Topic 7	
Topic 8	
Topic 9	
Topic 10	

And More ...

There's always more! To access the how-to videos that demonstrate the drills in my book, *Remarkable Speaking*, go to the Remarkable Framework playlist at <u>youtube.com/@</u> <u>remarkablespeaking</u> or scan the QR below.

VIDEO: HOW SOLOPRENEURS CAN FALL IN LOVE WITH USING SOCIAL MEDIA

Don't think that what you have to say is valuable? Interacting with your audience before you present your talk can override that fear - even if they are skeptical or disagree with your message. In this podcast, I offer the hosts a different perspective on what to say using social media—that, between the cat memes and advertisements, can be an incremental step to activating conversations that are meaningful and worthwhile. Check out the full episode of The Aspiring Solopreneur, Season 2, Episode 74.

 How Solopreneurs Can Fall in Love With Using Social Media

VIDEO: AN EXAMPLE OF INTERJECTION

Interrupting someone to keep the conversation on topic may sound rude. You can, however, respectfully assert your position by paraphrasing, a common strategy used in negotiations and conflict resolution.

To paraphrase, you repeat something that the person has said as your response. By acknowledging the person and what they've said, you show your interest, and they feel heard. A great example of this technique is an interview on "The Treatment," an arts podcast by the NPR member station KCRW. Listen to the forty-second audio clip where host Elvis Mitchell interjects to pause his guest, actress, writer, and producer Diarra Kilpatrick.

 An Example of Interjection

VIDEO: AN EXERCISE THAT WILL MAKE YOU MEMORABLE

If you aim to improve your comprehension and be memorable as a speaker, use the Shelley Grinder: a drill consisting of timed sprints that quelches fluffy filler words and rambling, revealing just one fully crystallized message in minutes. You will find that you're actually more proficient with less time.

For an example of how this is done, listen to Episode 507 of the Networking Rx podcast with Frank Agin. This is the second part of a two-part interview where I coached the host live on his show using the Shelley Grinder.

▶ An Exercise That Will Make You Memorable

If you're curious to hear what Frank and I discussed in Part One, listen to Networking Rx Episode 506:

▶ The Story That Attracts Others to You

VIDEO: TED TALKS

Some of the world's most compelling speakers express emotion. As a speaker, you're sharing your opinions and ideas because they have meaning to you. You can experience this by watching TED Talks where speakers share their life-altering moments and lessons learned. You'll notice their journeys are *filled with emotion*.

For an example, tune into these three of the top twenty-five most-watched TED Talks of all time (ted.com/playlists/171/the_most_popular_ted_talks_of_all_time). What is it about each one that you connect to?

▶ My Stroke of Insight, by Dr. Jill Bolte Taylor

▶ My Philosophy for a Happy Life, by Sam Berns

▶ The Power of Vulnerability, Dr. Brené Brown

SPEAKING PROMPTS

Speaking prompts are powerful cues for enhancing your communications. They help you to maintain focus, clearly articulate your message, and suggest transitions between different ideas making your speech more cohesive.

Choose a prompt from the categories below that best fits your message.

"I" Prompts

Lead off your talk with "I" prompts to get a clear direction and speak about the necessary details of your story instead of summarizing.

- There was a time when I ...
- I remember the moment ...
- I once had to ...
- Something unexpected happened when I ...
- In my experience as a ...
- One thing I'll never forget is ...
- I felt ...
- I told myself to ...

Don't Know What to Say Prompts

When you don't know how to answer unexpected questions, use these prompts to gracefully respond and share knowledge about things you do know with credibility.

- Thank you for bringing this to my attention. I don't have the right answer right now, but I will check with the team and get back to you. Here's what I do know ...
- I don't know much about that, but I can tell you this ...

- What a great question, it reminds of …
- I'm not following, can you tell me more about the time when …
- I haven't experienced that, but you might be surprised to hear …
- I'm not entirely sure, but there's a case study that says …
- I don't have the exact answer, however I've done something like …
- I'm not familiar with that topic, but I am curious if it is similar to …

Interjection Prompts

Interjecting is helpful when you're moderating a discussion or someone is dominating a conversation. These prompts politely bring the conversation back on track while giving others in the group a chance to participate.

- I agree with (name of person interrupting), and I'd also like to add …
- I hadn't thought of that, and it brings me to another point …
- Hold that thought (name of person interrupting). I'd love to know if the group is interested in learning more about this idea.
- What you're saying is really interesting, but I have another call. May we continue the discussion this afternoon?
- I want to dig deeper into that, but for the sake of time, I'd like to direct the conversation to …
- Up to this time, we've discussed (topic), let's now turn our attention to …
- I'd like to shift the focus and invite those who haven't contributed their ideas yet …
- I want to recap what we've said so far and then propose …

Slow Down Prompts

Try these prompts to slow down your speech when you sense that you're talking too fast or rambling. They guide you to ground your energy, regroup your thoughts, and return to the topic at hand.

- On second thought, I'll say …
- Let me break it down this way …
- Before we take a deep dive, I want to share …
- To put it more simply …

- I'd like to think of it in these terms …
- Let me rephrase that …
- Give me a moment to collect my thoughts …
- Let me circle back to my original idea …

Conviction Prompts

Reinforce your big idea with conviction prompts and deliver your message powerfully, with purpose and intention.

- I believe …
- My purpose in sharing this …
- Why I feel strongly about …
- My goal for our discussion …
- The reason I'm sharing this with you is…
- I've come to realize …
- Ultimately, the message I want to convey is …
- I deeply care about …

Value Prompts

Add value to any presentation by replacing generic features and benefits jargon with a learning moment. By using these prompts, you can express your unique perspective and explain why what you're sharing is important to you.

- It's important for me to tell you …
- An interesting lesson that I learned …
- The valuable takeaway is …
- What I love about my work is …
- In my experience, I …
- I've seen firsthand how …
- My journey has taught me …
- I hope my story has left you with a new perspective on …

Call To Action Prompts

Stay connected and build relationships with your audience. Whether you want them to make a purchase, sign up for a newsletter or just learn something new, call to action prompts wrap up your talk and open the door for the next conversation.

- Here's what I believe we can do …

- This is what I'm suggesting …

- Imagine …

- I invite you to …

- Many of my clients have had success with …

- May I email you the fact sheet (or white paper) with more information about the topic we discussed today?

- Join my workshop on (date), and experience my framework first-hand.

- Scan the QR code in the handout to access my free speaking resource (or newsletter), and let me know if you find it helpful.

- It has been a pleasure to have you as a guest on our podcast. We'd love to invite you back to the show!

- Subscribe to my YouTube channel and ring the bell to get reminders when I post new training videos and pro tips.

- Sign up for my Three-Day Challenge to Confidence (any challenge as it relates to the subject matter).

- For all attendees who joined the seminar today, email me a recording of your un-pitch for personalized feedback.

- Connect with me on LinkedIn, and weigh in on the conversation.

- Text me for Part Two of the webinar series. There's more to unpack from what we covered today in Part One.

PRO TIP: When you're feeling doubtful, start with I believe …

PRO TIP: Use "I," "me," or "my" language to make it specific to your experience versus speaking in vague references such as "you" or "we."

PRO TIP: When lost for words or need a moment to collect your thoughts, take a breath!

STORY BANK

If you're struggling to come up with something to talk about, create a story bank and speak with spontaneity. A story bank is a collection of interchangeable stories such as, mic-drop moments, your lived experiences, examples that you've read, anecdotes you've heard, quotes you like, relevant case studies, or industry news that someone told you about. These narratives are the content that you can use for any speaking event like a presentation, sales pitch, or interview. Additionally, I've included a list of interview questions in this section.

To build a story bank, use the worksheet on page 27 and instructions that follow.

Set a timer for one minute and make a list of your moments you've experienced in the last twenty-four hours. Your experiences don't have to be revolutionary, just random things that come to mind. Don't write them out in detail, simply make a list using brief descriptors. For example:

- Quarterly review with board of directors.
- Met a friend for lunch.
- Software implementation for the finance department.
- I broke my favorite sunglasses.

Next, choose one of the moments from your worksheet. Set a timer for one minute and start talking about it. Speak like yourself as you recall it happening and free your mind from structure.

Now choose another moment, set the timer and talk about it. Repeat these steps until you've talked through all your moments.

PRO TIP: Use "I," "me," or "my" language to make it specific to your experience versus speaking in vague references such as "you" or "we." You'll find a full list of prompts in the Speaking Prompts section of this workbook.

Interview Questions

Not sure how to handle interview questions? Build a story bank! Talking about your experiences reveals your interpersonal skills, conveys your understanding of the role and your suitability for it.

Set a one-minute timer, choose a question from the list that follows and speak your answer out loud. Next, add your experience to your Story Bank worksheet.

- Tell me about yourself?
- How do you define success?
- What are the advantages and disadvantages of working in a hybrid environment?
- How would you present a situation where a project was incomplete and the deadline had lapsed?
- If a team member consistently underperforms, what strategies would you implement to improve their performance?
- Describe a time when you faced a significant failure or setback. How did you overcome it?
- How would you explain a complex technical concept to a non-technical person?
- What do you do to stay up-to-date with industry trends and best practices?
- Why do you think you're the right candidate for this position?
- Where do you see yourself in the future in this organization?
- What do you love about the work you do?
- What do you look for in a company culture?

You might really want the job, but it's equally important that the company culture is a good fit for you. Think of your ideal work scenario and build a story bank of questions that you can ask the interviewer.

- How does this role contribute to future-focused initiatives for the organization?
- Can you tell me about the opportunities for professional development and growth within this role?
- How does the company conduct work-life balance and employee well-being?
- What advice would you give to someone new to this role?

STORY BANK WORKSHEET

Story 1	
Story 2	
Story 3	
Story 4	
Story 5	
Story 6	
Story 7	
Story 8	
Story 9	
Story 10	

CRANBERRY EFFECT

The key to speaking with clarity and authenticity is getting specific about the details. A summary gives you an overview, but you don't get any of the expressive details that help you connect with audiences. This drill will help you describe your experiences as you remember them happening and avoid rambling. You'll find it easier to access your words and speak naturally, just like when you speak in casual conversations.

Follow these steps to experience the Cranberry Effect, or scan the QR code below to watch my video tutorial on the Remarkable Framework playlist (youtube.com/@remarkablespeaking), where I'll guide you through the process.

 The Cranberry Effect

Get seated in a comfortable position on the floor or in a chair. Pick up an object that's in your current surroundings. It can be anything, a pen, your computer mouse, or a pair of glasses. Set a timer for five minutes. Next, look at the object and observe. Really study it carefully, looking closely at the details.

What do you see?

Why do you have this object?

When did you last use it?

What was happening at that moment?

Keep looking. What else do you see?

As you reflect on these details, perhaps you begin to think of moments that you haven't thought of in a long time, and, surprisingly, they come flooding back to your memory. These are the visceral qualities I want you to reveal when you're looking at the object. Ask yourself these questions, and let your mind wander.

> PRO TIP: Don't summarize because the details help to tell the story and explain your point.

> PRO TIP: Use 'I,' 'me,' or 'my' language to bypass structuring how you tell the story and simply talk about it as you would in casual conversation.

> PRO TIP: Tap into your bodily senses to revisit the moment experientially. Can you visualize the room? Do you smell the aromas? What sounds do you hear? What kind of movements are you experiencing? Was there a sweetness to the taste or a texture to the touch that prompts you to reveal the moment?

I AM STATEMENTS

To convey empathy and understanding to your audience, talk about experiences where you've succeeded and failed. As a leader, you can demonstrate the value of your journey while creating a safe space for others to learn without judgment.

There are three I AM worksheets in this section: I Succeeded At, I Failed At, and My Coworker. After you complete the drills, add the statements to the Story Bank worksheet on page 27.

I Succeeded At …

What sets you apart from others in your profession? Talking about your successes, like the moment you founded your company or how you led the team to complete a challenging project, people recognize your distinctive qualities and unique methods for getting things done.

Set a timer for two minutes and write out the entire statement that follows, listing as many successes as you can.

I am good at _____ because I succeeded at _____.

For example:

I am good at *coaching executives* because I succeeded at *listening to what they are not saying to help them achieve their speaking potential*.

> PRO TIP: Your work is routine, you're very skilled at what you do, and it's true, so you can write without judgment.

Write your success statements here:

_____

_____

_____

_____

_____

_____

_____

How did it feel to write out your successes? Pretty good, right?

Take a few seconds and reflect on the very moment you experienced one of your successes.

Take another few seconds and reflect on how that moment influenced your decision making today.

Next, speak each success statement out loud. Speaking each success out loud probably sounds and feels better than good.

I Failed At ...

There are many things you're skilled at today because of a past failure that served as a learning moment. By identifying your failures, you can comfortably talk about them in situations when someone catches you off guard with a challenging question.

Set a timer for two minutes and write out the entire statement that follows, listing as many failures as you can.

I am good at _____ because I failed at _____.

For example:

I am good at *recording authentic videos in minutes* because I failed at *trying to make a perfectly scripted video*.

Write your failure statements here:

_____

_____

_____

_____

_____

_____

_____

How did it feel to write out your failures?

Take a few seconds and reflect on the very moment you experienced one of your failures.

Take another few seconds and reflect on how that moment influenced your leadership style today.

Next, speak each failure statement out loud and recognize your moment of growth.

My Coworker ...

If you're looking to motivate your coworkers and teams, highlight their successes with a variation of the I AM statement. By promoting others, you acknowledge their contributions and reinforce mutual respect among colleagues.

Set a timer for two minutes and write out the entire statement that follows, listing as many successes for your coworkers as you can.

My coworker _____ is good at _____ because they succeeded at _____.

For example:

My coworker *Theo* is good at *closing the deal with prospects* because they succeeded at *presenting interactive demonstrations that make it a great experience*.

Write your coworker statements here:

_____

_____

_____

_____

_____

_____

_____

How did it feel to write out the successes of your coworker or team?

Take a few seconds and reflect on the very moment you experienced one of their successes.

Take another few seconds and reflect on how that moment impacted that individual, the department or company.

At your next meeting, speak each statement out loud and encourage a positive work environment.

SHELLEY GRINDER

Whether you're creating content for your speech, presentation, pitch, webinar, seminar, podcast, facilitation, meeting agenda, employee training, lunch and learn, panel discussion moderating, video recording, interview, social media post, toast, eulogy—essentially any type of speaking event, the Shelley Grinder will help you articulate your message in four minutes.

The Shelley Grinder is a series of speaking sprints repeated in successive rounds, inspired by the 'Sprint' methodology co-developed by Jake Knapp and John Zeratsky. The process of reducing the time of each sprint forces your brain to quickly get to the point, without rambling or overthinking. You'll find it even easier to speak more freely in your natural voice.

To see how it works, go to the Remarkable Framework playlist to watch the The Shelley Grinder video and listen to Episode 507 of the Networking Rx podcast with Frank Agin, An Exercise That Will Make You Memorable, where I coached the host live on his show.

▶ The Shelley Grinder

▶ An Exercise That Will Make You Memorable

Have a timer handy and your speech topic, or, as I call it in the Framework, your big idea. When doing the drill, don't worry about structuring the perfect statement, just allow your mind to freely explore wherever it wants to go, and make each sprint unique.

SPRINT 1: Set the timer for ninety seconds and talk about your big idea. What do you want your audience to know?

SPRINT 2: Set the timer for sixty seconds and grind your idea with more clarity; let new thoughts emerge.

SPRINT 3: Set the timer for thirty seconds and continue to grind your idea even more.

Were you able to crystallize your big idea from a ninety-second sprint into thirty seconds? If you are not yet clear on your big idea or feel you need to refine it a little more, repeat Sprints 1 through 3 of the drill and take note of the following pro tips.

PRO TIP: You're not memorizing a phrase, you're exploring different ways to express your big idea with each sprint; you might even surprise yourself at how quickly you can arrive at one very crystal clear answer.

PRO TIP: Do not use crafty taglines or industry jargon. Speak in "I," "me," or "my" language to access a real moment and talk like your natural self.

PRO TIP: If you need to protect the privacy of individuals or companies and proprietary information, you don't have to mention names. You can replace "Alphabet and Google's CEO Sundar Pichai" with "The CEO of an internet tech company."

For the fourth and final sprint in this drill, you want to repeat your big idea and end with your purpose to give context.

SPRINT 4: Set a timer for another sixty seconds and repeat your big idea—only this time use the full sixty seconds to speak in a relaxed and natural way, and end with your purpose. To do that, use a speaking prompt from the Speaking Prompts section; for example:

- I believe …
- The valuable takeaway is …
- Why I feel strongly about …
- My journey has taught me …

When your big idea can stand on its own in sixty seconds, you will be able to speak about it for ten minutes or two hours with greater focus, comfort, and confidence.

Repeat the Shelley Grinder for content that you added to your Story Bank worksheet on page 27. If you're developing a presentation or another type of speaking event, use the Shelley Grinder together with the Tree Grid and Evergreen tools in respective sections of this workbook. These tools are interconnected as one solution to structure your talk as described in my book, *Remarkable Speaking*.

TREE GRID

Creating content to support your key message in presentations can be daunting. You can use the Tree Grid tool from the framework to streamline content creation for your talk, eliminating the stress and frustration of endless drafts.

Tree Grid is an at-a-glance reference to collect all the elements you want to include in your speaking event; i.e., your big idea, supporting content, and call to action. You'll use the Shelley Grinder in tandem to clarify what to say, and write a brief descriptor for elements in **Sections A, B, C,** and **D** in the worksheet on page 39.

Start with **Sections A.** Refer to the Shelley Grinder section of this workbook to clarify your big idea. Then add it to the Tree Grid.

In **Section B**, you're going to set a timer for sixty seconds and for this step, write a list of your supporting content that best explains your big idea. Supporting content are your interchangeable stories that can be mic-drop moments, your lived experiences, examples that you've read, anecdotes you've heard, quotes you like, relevant case studies, or industry news that someone told you about. These narratives are your go-to content for any speaking event such as a facilitation, sales pitch, or video recording.

Next, for each supporting content you wrote in **Section B**, set a timer for sixty seconds and write why it's important for you to share in **Section C**. What lesson have you learned from each moment? What value does each experience have for your audience? Think about how each story connects to your big idea.

At this stage, your Tree Grid worksheet is filling up with the elements of your speech: your big idea and all your supporting content. Choose one piece of content listed from **Section B** and its counterpart in **Section C**, and use the Shelley Grinder on page 35 to articulate your thoughts. Repeat the Shelley Grinder for all of your content in **Sections B** and **C**.

Now that you've got your big idea and supporting content, what do you want your audience to do about it? Ask them with a call to action. You may not be selling anything for purchase per se, but you are sharing information. Your call to action is an opportunity to connect with people and nurture future relationships.

Follow the steps for the Shelley Grinder with one of these prompts to guide you:

- Here's what I believe we can do …

- I invite you to …

- Connect with me on LinkedIn, and ...

- Imagine …

When you can successfully convey your call to action, write it in **Section D** of the worksheet.

TREE GRID WORKSHEET

Section D
My Call to Action
What action do you want your audience to take for your big idea?

Section B **What Is My Supporting Content?** What moments, experiences, examples, anecdotes, data, case studies, industry news, and so on best explain your big idea in Section A?	Section C **Why Am I Sharing This Content?** For each piece of content listed in Section B, write why it is important for you to share. What lesson have you learned or what value does this have for your audience?
1B	1C
2B	2C
3B	3C
4B	4C
5B	5C
6B	6C

Section A
My Big Idea
What do you want your audience to know?

You'll discover that the Remarkable Framework is universal because its reliable tools can help you in any speaking situation. For example, you can make meetings more productive and engaging. Distribute copies of the Tree Grid variation that follows and have people brainstorm solutions to solve an issue with sixty-second writing sprints at different stages of the agenda.

TREE GRID WORKSHEET

Section D
Call to Action
What action is a possible solution for the problem?

Section B
What Is the Supporting Content?
What moments, experiences, examples, anecdotes, data, case studies, industry news, and so on best explain the problem in Section A?

1B

2B

3B

Section C
Why Share This Content?
For each piece of content in Section B, list why it is important to share. What is the lesson learned or what value does this have for solving the problem?

1C

2C

3C

Section A
Big Idea
What is the problem we are trying to solve?

EVERGREEN

Structuring presentations is often challenging and time-intensive, especially given their dynamic nature. The Framework's Evergreen tool designed to help you organize the most necessary content for your speech, thereby strengthening the impact of your big idea.

How does the structure of your speech resemble that of an evergreen? Like a comprehensive speech, a tree symbolizes balance and harmony and the interconnectedness of everything.

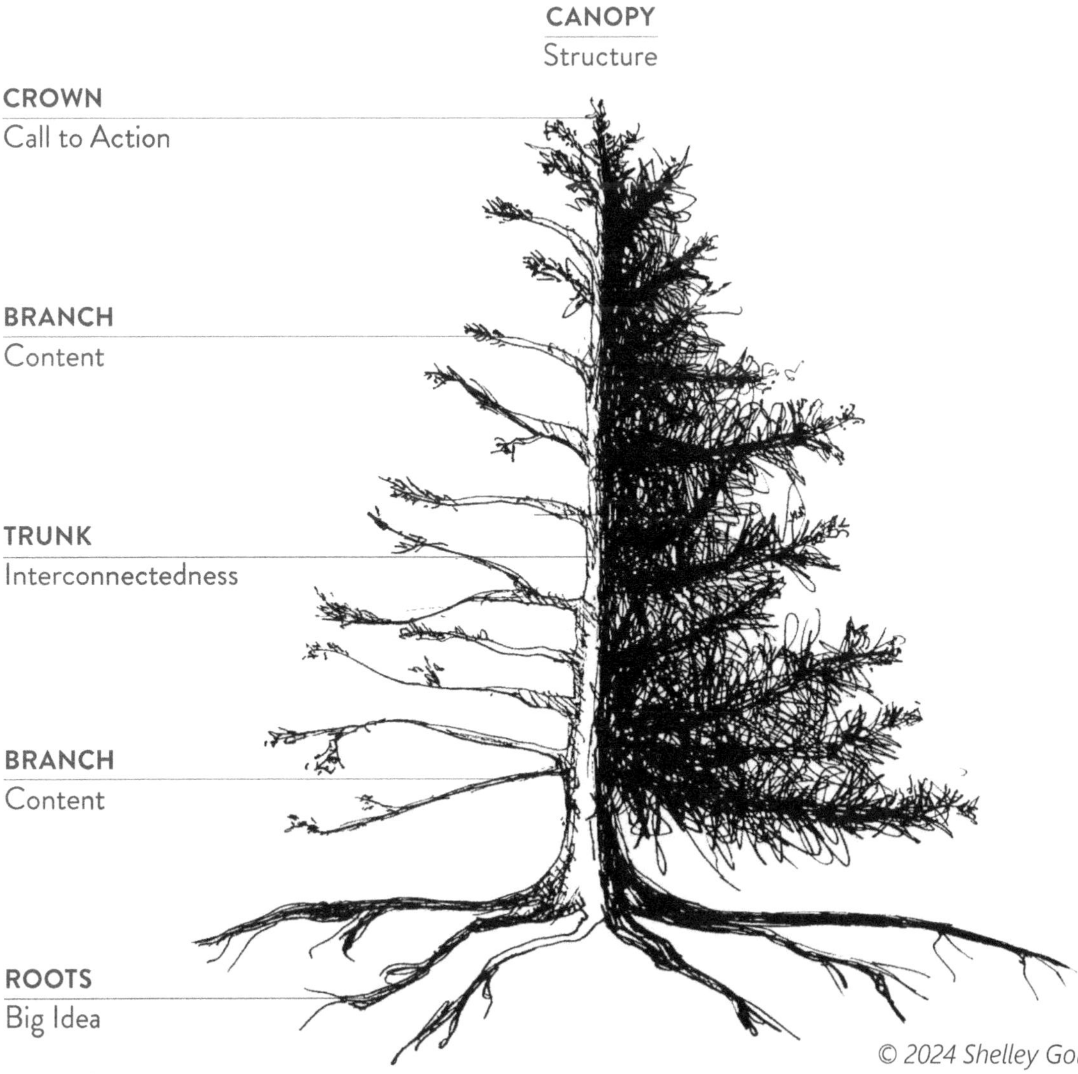

CANOPY
Structure

CROWN
Call to Action

BRANCH
Content

TRUNK
Interconnectedness

BRANCH
Content

ROOTS
Big Idea

Firmly grounded like tree roots, your big idea anchors the structure of your speech.

The trunk interconnects all the parts of the tree to balance the tree's structure. By repeating your big idea, you reinforce your message, connecting all the elements of your speech. The repetition helps your audience to understand and retain your big idea.

The branches of a tree are the lifelines that help to create the tree's canopy, its distinct shape, in the same way that your supporting content helps to bring your big idea into clear view.

The crown that nurtures the Evergreen is the call to action that wraps up your speech, providing an opportunity to encourage your audience to take action.

Looking at the Evergreen worksheet on page 43, you'll notice that **Sections A, B/C,** and **D** correlate with the sections on the Tree Grid. Now you have a visual for how to organize the elements of your speech from the root to the crown: your big idea, supporting content, and call to action.

Write your big idea and call to action from the Tree Grid in **Sections A** and **D** on the Evergreen worksheet.

Next, write each story on a small Post-it® and add them to the **B/C Sections** of the Evergreen. The bottom of the tree is the beginning of your speech and, filling in content working your way to the top, your call to action is the wrap up.

As you add and move your content around the Evergreen, be sure all your moments, experiences, examples, anecdotes, data, case studies, or industry news reinforce your big idea. If the content doesn't reinforce what it is you want to say, archive it in your story bank for another talk. *Always bring the conversation back to your big idea.*

PRO TIP: Throughout your talk, repeat your big idea a lot and often. This is really valuable when you're presenting complex subjects and bigger scale ideas.

PRO TIP: If you have so many Post-its® on the Evergreen that you can no longer see the tree, that's a sign that you probably have too much content.

PRO TIP: Wrap things up, and say your call to action with conviction. A weak ending would be like a sentence without a period.

EVERGREEN

To learn how to apply the Framework like determining the timeliness of speeches, strategies to tackle memorization, how to get the call back, and other presentation tips, refer to Chapters 8 and 9 in my book, *Remarkable Speaking*. With its universal applications, you'll discover the Remarkable Framework endures, standing the test of time. It's evergreen.

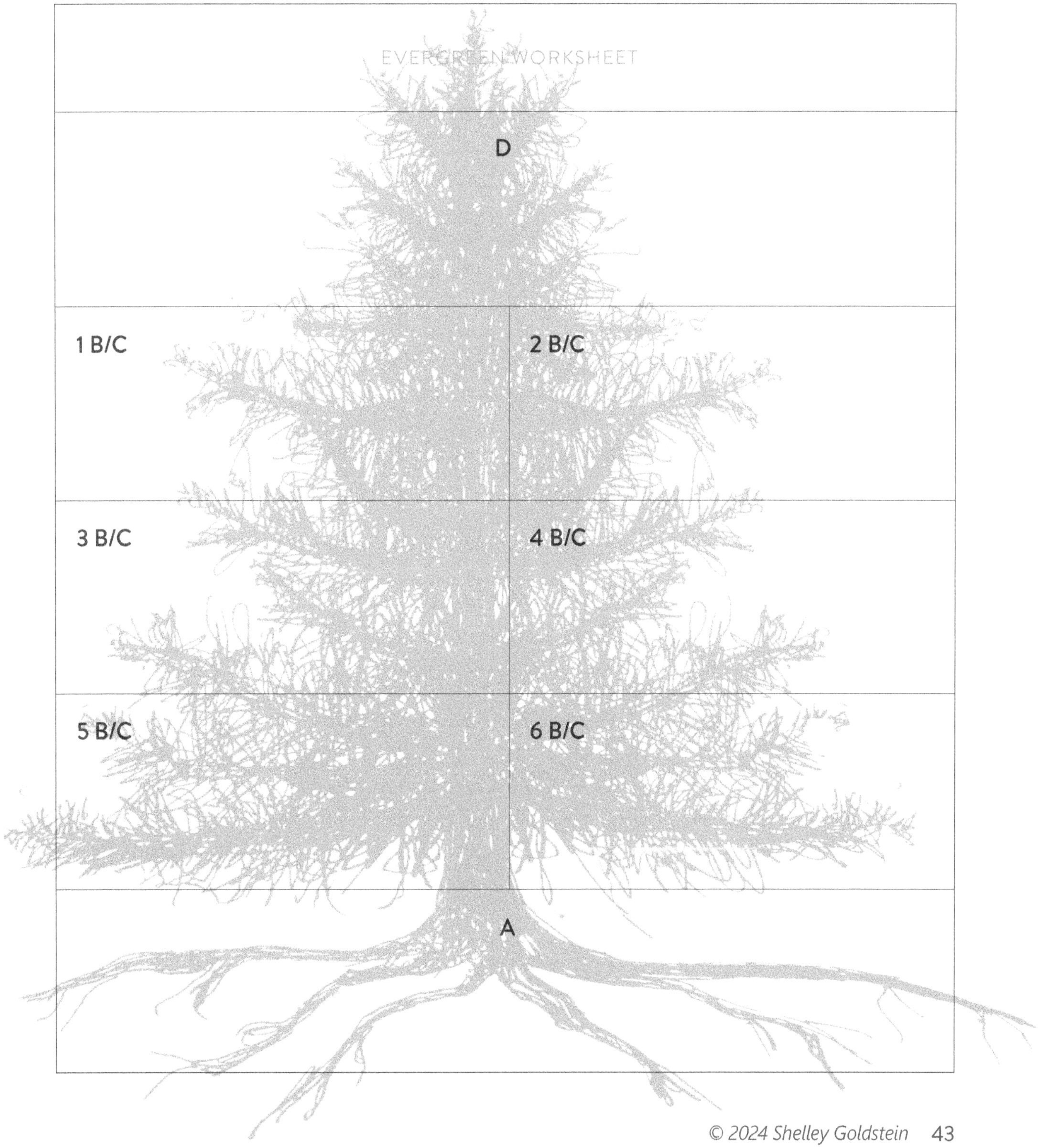
EVERGREEN WORKSHEET
D
1 B/C
2 B/C
3 B/C
4 B/C
5 B/C
6 B/C
A

KEY TAKEAWAYS

Reading my book *Remarkable Speaking*, I had you write your key takeaways at the conclusion of each chapter to reinforce what you've learned, strengthen neural pathways, and motivate you to keep speaking.

Each chapter is named after the acronym, R.E.M.A.R.K.A.B.L.E., with each letter focusing on the development of core skills that directly translate into results. You can use this space for additional takeaways you observed as your personalized Remarkable Framework guide.

CHAPTER 1: REFRAME
Get out of your head.

_____

_____

_____

_____

CHAPTER 2: EMPOWER
Take ownership of what you believe.

_____

_____

_____

_____

CHAPTER 3: MIC-DROP MOMENT

Let your emotions transcend your words.

_____

_____

_____

_____

CHAPTER 4: ACTIVATE

Step into the spotlight!

_____

_____

_____

_____

CHAPTER 5: REFLECT AND REVEAL

Explore self-expression.

_____

_____

_____

_____

CHAPTER 6: KEEP QUIET

Give silence a voice.

_____

_____

_____

_____

CHAPTER 7: ARTICULATE
Clarify and bring your big idea to life.

_____

_____

_____

_____

CHAPTER 8: BE THE BRIDGE, NOT THE BARRIER
Have conversations that connect.

_____

_____

_____

_____

CHAPTER 9: LEVERAGE YOUR MESSAGE
Transfer your skills for excellence.

_____

_____

_____

_____

CHAPTER 10: EMBODY
Manifest confidence and speak remarkably.

_____

_____

_____

_____

SPEAKING SURVIVAL CHECKLIST

A checklist of speaking principles can help reduce stress and boost confidence before your next talk. It serves as a quick reminder to stay focused on what's important so you can be more productive as a speaker.

Check the list, then let go and talk about what you know.

- ☐ Every opportunity to speak is an opportunity to have a conversation.

- ☐ If you're feeling nervous, reframe that thought to "I am excited!"

- ☐ If someone says they had a good day, be curious and ask them what made it good.

- ☐ Take a breath. The breath gives you space, separating turbulence from clarity.

- ☐ If you want to warm up, do some Power Up drills and speak up.

- ☐ If you feel doubtful, own your thoughts with "I believe."

- ☐ If the audience looks too big, have conversations and engage in a few icebreakers before things kick off.

- ☐ If you make a mistake, turn it into a relatable commonality by making it part of the conversation.

- ☐ If you feel uncomfortable, do it again so it will become more familiar.

- ☐ If you're caught up with too many technical cues, repeat a few tongue twisters and get out of your head.

- ☐ If you want to create a buzz with your speaking, record a video to reply to an email or text.

- ☐ If someone is hogging the conversation, interject and hand off to the group to make it a great experience.

☐ When you give your introduction, share a mic-drop moment and stand out from the crowd.

☐ If you catch yourself summarizing, use a speaking prompt with "I," "me," or "my" language to get to a real moment.

☐ If you feel like you're speaking too fast, manage your energy with a few breaths to slow down.

☐ When you find yourself rambling and trailing off topic, use a speaking prompt; you'll come back much stronger.

☐ If you're struggling to connect with your big idea, use the Shelley Grinder to eliminate extraneous details and articulate your words.

☐ If you're at a loss for words, tap into your story bank and talk about what you know.

☐ If you're pressed for time writing the outline for your talk, sprint to save time.

☐ If the circumstances for your talk change, revisit the Evergreen to edit and adapt.

SPEAKING RESOURCES

You now have the tools to make practice a requirement and speak with confidence. Keep the conversations going and explore these additional resources to contribute to your success.

Download your free tip guides and learn my methods for creating compelling slide decks, strategies from elite athletes to improve your speeches, pitfalls to avoid when presenting, and other solutions.

Never miss a single pro tip—subscribe to my social channels! Scan the QR code below to access my Linktree (linktr.ee/shelleygoldstein), where you can click on each icon to stay up to date on new releases. You'll find my public speaking how-tos, informational videos, upcoming speaking events and workshops, *The Remarkable Podcast*, and so much more!

Here's to your remarkable conversations to come!

www.ingramcontent.com/pod-product-compliance
Lightning Source LLC
Chambersburg PA
CBHW041154120626

46547CB00020B/3213